W9-DHS-827

The Talking Tree

Created by

Al Cherry

Written by

Rita McKenzie

Illustrated by

Terence Hanley

Edited by

Elizabeth Kutzko
Beth Jester
Al Cherry

Dedication: I would like to acknowledge my wife, Beth, my parents, Charles & Winifred Cherry, and my children, Dale, Beth and Tricia, for encouraging me to listen to how trees communicate. Also to my eight grandchildren; Jim, Patrick, Christopher, Matthew, Joclyn, Jennifer, Nicholas, & Christine for listening to my stories of *The Talking Tree*.

Trees stretched their branches up into the bright blue summer sky. The morning sunlight glistened off the softly moving emerald leaves. Tina smiled at them from her open bedroom window. It was her first day in a new neighborhood. Birds flitted from branch to branch. Their chirps and warbles merged with the bark of the neighbor's dog. A newspaper flopped onto the front door step. Doors slammed. Voices carried on distant conversations. The trees creaked and mumbled. Their words were lost in the shuffle of morning sounds.

"Hello, Oak," said Maple, its roots firmly planted in Tina's yard.   An orange and white spotted cat crawled up onto one of its branches.

"Why, good morning, Maple," replied Oak in the yard next door. "Yes, it is quite nice. I see you have a new furry friend. Does it belong to your new owners?"

Maple stretched out its limb. The cat curled his speckled paws beneath himself and closed his eyes to sleep. "Yes, it does," it replied. "I haven't met the rest of the family yet. I hope they know how to listen to us."

"I'm sure Jenny will fill them in. It's been a pleasure standing in her yard," Oak said. It flexed its limbs proudly and shook its handsome leaves.

The door to Maple's house opened, and Tina ran out into the yard. She hesitated for a moment. The air seemed full of life. It smelled rich and musty like a distant forest and freshly mowed lawns. As she stepped into the shade of Maple, a boy and a girl ran up the street. She hesitated for a moment, but they ran right up to her.

"I'm Jocelyn," said the girl. "You just moved in yesterday, huh?"

"Yes, we did," said Tina. "I'm Tina."

"I'm Patrick," said the boy. "We are going to Jenny's to get cookies. Want to come with us?"

"Who's Jenny?" asked Tina.

"She lives right next door to you," Jocelyn said. "She bakes cookies on Saturdays, and she's a lot of fun. She talks to trees."

Tina hesitated for a moment. She wasn't sure she should be eating cookies made by someone who talks to trees.

"It's all right," said Patrick. "Our parents know we're here. Jocelyn keeps telling me about talking trees. That sounds nutty to me, but I thought I'd finally join Jocelyn in eating some of those cookies."

"Sure!" Tina exclaimed. This sounded like a great way to start exploring her new neighborhood. The three grinned at each other, and then they headed off to follow the smell of freshly baked cookies to Jenny's house.

As the children ran up to the house, a tall woman came out with a picnic basket in one hand and a plate of cookies in the other. She smiled broadly and said, "Good morning, Jocelyn! Who are your friends?"

"This is Tina and Patrick. I told them that trees talk to you, Jenny, but they don't believe me," Jocelyn said.

"I'm glad I put extra glasses in the picnic basket," Jenny said laughing. "It is such a beautiful day. I thought we should have our cookies outside." She handed the plate to Jocelyn.

They settled on the lawn underneath Oak, and Jenny pulled glasses and a milk jug out of the basket. She asked, "So none of you have heard trees talk?" She winked at Jocelyn who smiled back. Tina and Patrick shook their heads. "That's not a surprise," she continued. "Not everyone can hear them, but arborists can."

"What do you mean 'arborist?'" Patrick asked.

"I'm an arborist," Jenny said. She poured a glass of milk for everyone. "'Arbor' comes from Latin, and it means 'tree'. I take care of trees in the urban forest."

"An urban forest, what's that?" asked Patrick as Jocelyn handed him the plate.

"It's trees that grow in a city. I teach people how to plant trees around their houses and keep them healthy after they're planted," Jenny said.

"How do you keep them healthy?" Tina asked. It was her turn with the plate. She carefully picked out a medium-sized one, and it felt warm and soft in her hand. She passed the plate on to Jenny.

"I care for them in a special way. I listen to them, and I teach others how to listen, too. That's what an arborist does," Jenny said as she set the plate down on the grass.

"That sounds neat," said Patrick. "How did you learn that?"

"Well, Patrick," Jenny said, "when I was about your age, I lived in a house with a beautiful, big oak in the front yard—something like this one. One hot summer day I lay down under it and stared up at the leaves. I noticed they looked funny. They were droopy and dry. As I lay there looking at them, I heard a faint whispering sound. I yawned, and the whispering grew louder and louder. I saw lots of colors, shades, and shapes as the wind blew the rustling leaves...."

"...Suddenly this voice said, 'I wish my leaves weren't so crispy.' I looked around, but I didn't see anyone. I had an older brother who liked to play tricks on me. At first I was sure it had to be him, but then a voice came right out of the trunk. It said, 'Yes, it's me... your favorite tree.'"

"What did you do?" asked Patrick.

"I made sure I was awake," said Jenny, winking at Jocelyn who started to giggle. "It was strange having the tree in my yard suddenly say something. The tree assured me this was nothing new, but I have to admit I was pretty surprised. It took me a few minutes to fully realize that it was really talking with me. And once it found its voice, it sure wanted to talk. It told me all kinds of things that afternoon... things that I hadn't thought about before."

"What sort of things did the tree tell you?" asked Tina. She wasn't sure whether or not to believe in talking trees.

"Well, Tina," replied Jenny, "do you know that trees help your parents by making it cheaper for them to heat and cool their house?"

"How do they do that?" asked Tina.

"They provide shade in the summer which helps cool down the house, and they block the wind in the winter."

"I never thought of that," said Patrick. "What else did this tree tell you?"

"He told me about this neat thing trees do for us," said Jenny. "They provide oxygen for us to breathe."

"How do trees do that?" asked Patrick.

"Well, Patrick," replied Jenny, "it said that trees take the carbon dioxide that we breathe out and put out oxygen which we need to breathe in. They take carbon dioxide and soak up energy from sunlight to make carbohydrates so they can grow. That's how trees make food, and it's called photosynthesis. We need oxygen, and they need carbon dioxide. We need each other."

"What else did the tree say?" asked Jocelyn. She smiled broadly and took another bite of her cookie.

Jenny smiled back at her and continued, "The tree told me there were all kinds of complicated things taking place inside of it. It's hard to imagine that by looking at a tree."

The children shook their heads in agreement. Jenny offered everyone more cookies. Patrick and Jocelyn each took one while Tina took two. The melting chocolate chips were too hard to resist.

"By this point, the tree was very happy to chatter away," Jenny continued. "It told me about all kinds of things we get from trees. It asked me what I'd had for dinner. When I mentioned an apple pie, it asked me if I knew where that came from. Do any of you know?"

"A grocery store?" asked Patrick.

"They have apples at a grocery store, but they were first part of a tree," Jenny replied. "A lot of the things we use were once part of a tree. Your bed and chairs in your room and even your closet doors are all made of wood. Even part of that car in your parent's driveway came from trees."

"Oh, come on. I know metal doesn't come from trees!" Patrick said.

"No, but the rubber used to make the tires comes from trees."

"Really?" asked Patrick. "What else?"

"We get lots of things from trees," Jenny continued. "There's medicine like aspirin…. the paper in books, cork for school bulletin boards, and even the pencils you write with. It would be impossible to list everything. Many of the things we use were first part of a tree. That's why we need to take good care of our trees, and this is also why the tree in my yard wanted to talk to me. You see, trees are used to growing in forests. They don't mind being in the city, but it's harder for them to grow there because the conditions aren't the same as in a forest."

"But why would a tree talk to you about that?" asked Jocelyn.

"Because we need to help them get the things they need to be healthy.   At first I couldn't imagine that I could do anything to help. The tree was so much bigger than I was. It didn't look very happy though with its leaves curled. When I asked it what I could do, it told me to look at the ground under its canopy."

"Its what?" asked Tina.

"Canopy... a canopy is the top part of a tree, its leaves and branches. It's all the things you see when you look up in a tree or in a forest. The tree wanted me to look at the ground underneath its leaves and branches. If you look around at all the trees in our yards, you see mostly grass, right?"

The children all nodded.

"The tree explained to me that when you are in a natural forest, the ground doesn't look like this," said Jenny. "The floor of a forest is covered with leaves, small branches and other things that have fallen from above. The tree demanded to know what had happened to all of its leaves!"

"We rake up all of our leaves," said Patrick, "and put them in garbage bags."

"So did we," said Jenny, "until I had this talk with the tree....."

"…..It explained to me that those leaves and twigs have things in them trees need called nutrients," Jenny continued.

"What are those?" Tina asked.

"Nutrients are kind of like vitamins to a tree. They are tools that help the tree use food. The tree explained to me that there are small bugs and worms called decomposers. These decomposers break down the leaves, twigs, and pieces of bark into small bits. This returns the nutrients to the soil so that the roots of the tree can absorb them. From there, the nutrients travel up through the tree to the leaves and branches where it can use them. It's a natural cycle."

"So the leaves fall, and bugs chew them into little bits. That puts nutrients back in the soil. The roots pick up the nutrients. Those nutrients go through the tree to the leaves and branches. When leaves and branches fall off the tree, the bugs break them up again. Is that right?" asked Jocelyn.

"That's correct," said Jenny.

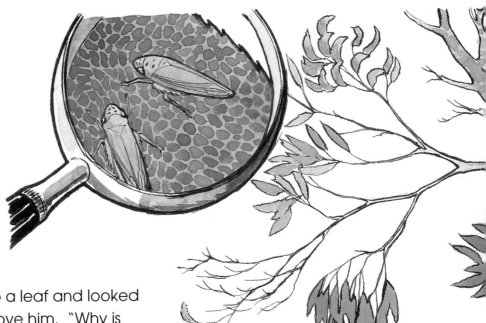

Patrick picked up a leaf and looked at the huge tree above him. "Why is that natural cycle so important?"

"The tree said that if it didn't get enough nutrients or water, its leaves get all droopy," Jenny said. "I felt bad, because its leaves were definitely brown and crunchy."

"You know how when you get sick a doctor will ask you what kind of symptoms you have," Jenny continued, "such as whether you are coughing or have an upset stomach? That's so the doctor can figure out what's wrong with you. Curled up leaves are the tree's way of coughing. The tree explained to me that when its leaves look like that, it is showing that it is suffering and stressed. When that happens, harmful insects and diseases can attack it, and it won't have the energy to fight them."

"What could you do to help the tree?" asked Tina.

"The tree explained to me that it needed to be treated as if it were in a forest," Jenny said. "That meant using the leaves as mulch. Rather than raking them up, they could be left on the ground to naturally return the nutrients to the soil. It also said that the leaves keep water from evaporating and provided a home for those tiny bugs."

"I guess we shouldn't throw our leaves away," Tina said. "You can learn a lot from trees."

"You sure can," said Jenny.

"How different is it for a tree in a forest?" asked Patrick.

"In the forest, a tree has lots of company. There are many different kinds of trees. Some are big, and some are small. In the shade of the canopy grow smaller trees, bushes and other plants. This is called the understory."

"The tree told you all of that?" asked Patrick.

Jenny laughed and said, "It did seem to talk a lot."

"So a forest kind of has layers?" asked Tina.

"That's right," said Jenny. "The tree said that because of all those layers, the trees and other plants are protected from wind, heat, and cold. It's a lot different for a tree standing all by itself in a yard. It's even worse if it's next to a house."

"How does a house make it worse?" asked Tina.

"The sun reflects off the house and makes it hotter for the tree."

"You mean it could get sunburned?" asked Patrick. "I got sunburned a couple of weeks ago, and it really hurt."

"It's similar…," said Jenny.
"The heat bouncing off the house
makes the air warmer which causes a tree's
leaves to wither and brown on the edges. The
tree told me that in a forest it's much cooler. All the
trees and bushes cut down the heat of the sun. Have
you ever walked in a forest?"

"I have," said Jocelyn. "It was cooler."

"It may be 10 degrees cooler inside the forest rather
than outside."

"What else did he say about a forest?" asked Patrick.

"We were interrupted at that point," said Jenny. "My older brother came up in his car and drove underneath the tree to park in the driveway. He hopped out of the car and ran into the house without even saying a word."

"He sounds mean," said Tina.

"I don't think he meant to be, but the tree screamed when he drove up. When I asked what was wrong, the tree told me the car hurt it."

"How did the car hurt it?" asked Tina. "It didn't hit the trunk."

"That was something else the tree was trying to tell me," said Jenny. "It had me look way up into the top branches, and I noticed that there were some bare branches right in the middle of a bunch of leaves. He told me those were because of the car."

"But how could the car do that?" asked Patrick. "You can't tell me the car was anywhere near the top of the tree."

"Oh, no!" Jenny said laughing. "How do you think nutrients get from the roots to the leaves?"

"Through the trunk and branches," said Jocelyn.

"You've heard this story before," Jenny said with a smirk. "Have a couple more cookies." While the children grabbed more from the plate, she continued, "Trees have special transport systems inside them called xylem and phloem. You know how I said that the roots absorb nutrients?"

The children mumbled and nodded since their mouths were full of cookies.

"The tree explained that the xylem moves the water and nutrients up to its leaves," Jenny continued. "Then the phloem moves sugar produced in its leaves by photosynthesis to other parts of the tree."

"What do you think happens if a tree's roots can't get any nutrients?" Jenny asked.

The children thought for a moment, chewing rapidly. Tina suddenly swallowed hard and exclaimed, "Those branches you saw that didn't have any leaves died from lack of water and nutrients!"

"Yes!" Jenny said. "Part of that was because of the weight of the car. The tree told me that when cars and other heavy equipment sit on the ground underneath a tree's canopy, the soil gets compacted or smashed down. This doesn't usually happen to a tree in the forest."

"Why not?" asked Patrick.

"Normally forest soil is light and soft," explained Jenny. "A tree's roots easily work their way through the soil to gather all the water and nutrients it needs to grow."

"But if roots are so deep, how can something like a car smash them?" asked Tina.

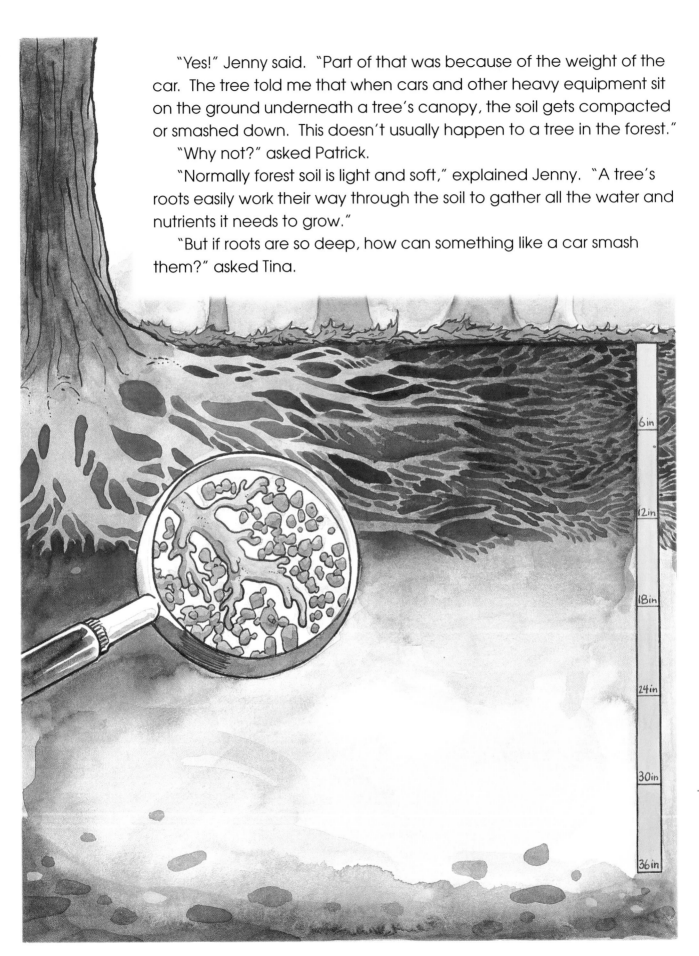

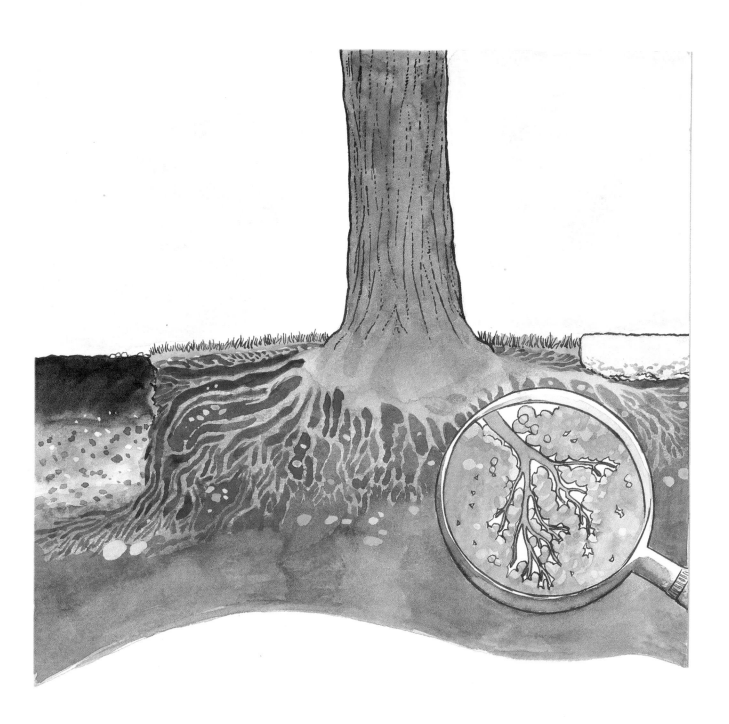

"A tree's roots are in the top 18 inches of soil," said Jenny.

"I always thought they were much deeper in the ground," Patrick said.

"So did I," Jenny said. "The tree called that the 'Deep Root Fable.'"

"Is there anything we can do to keep tree roots from getting squashed?" asked Patrick.

"Do you remember the mulch I told you about?" asked Jenny.

The children nodded.

"That will help. It'll protect the soil and roots by letting people know the ground around the base of a tree is important. Vehicles shouldn't park there," she said. "Mulch can help prevent another problem too. The tree showed me rips and tears on its trunk just above the grass."

"How did those get there?" asked Tina.

"I didn't know either," replied Jenny, "but the tree reminded me that my brother cut the grass the week before to earn his allowance. He nicked the trunk with a weed whacker, because the grass grew right up to it."

"How are you suppose to cut the grass around the tree?" asked Patrick.

"The tree said that grass doesn't need to grow right next to the trunk," Jenny said. "If I put mulch under its canopy, it would protect the bark from being torn and prevent roots near the top of the soil from being cut by the lawn mower."

"It would hurt to get sliced up with one of those things," Jocelyn said.

"Yes," said Jenny, "and the tree pointed out that the bark protects all those transport systems that carry nutrients and water up and down in the tree. You know what would happen if the bark were cut all the way around the trunk?"

The children thought for a bit, and finally Patrick guessed, "it would cut off the transport of food and water up and down the tree?"

"That's right," Jenny said grimly. "The tree would die. In the forest there are animals that eat small plants, but none of them hurt a tree like lawnmowers and weed whackers."

"But we can prevent that from happening by listening to trees, right?" asked Tina.

"All you have to do is pay attention to its leaves, branches, bark and roots to see if it's healthy and take care of it as if it were in the forest," Jenny said.

"Is that sort of like being a doctor of trees?" asked Patrick.

"That's what I do," replied Jenny. "I decided after talking to the tree that I wanted to look after trees and help them stay healthy."

"I want to be a tree doctor, too!" exclaimed Patrick.

"I definitely want trees to talk to me," Tina said.

"That's what I decided too, because from then on," said Jenny, "I wanted to listen to trees and take care of them. I studied trees in the urban forest, and I became an arborist. I learned that the more you know about trees, the more they will tell you."

"Did the tree really talk to you, Jenny?" asked Patrick.

Jenny beamed, "Trees don't talk to us in words. If you pay attention to all the parts of a tree and look for clues, they will tell you what they need."

"I know that a tree planted in a city," Jenny continued, "needs to be treated like it was in a forest. I give it the mulch it needs to replace nutrients and protect the bark, and I plant trees in groups like in the forest. I pay attention to the leaves, the branches, the roots, and the bark. That's how the tree talks to me. Trees in the urban forest need special care, and we can all help by listening to them."

"How about another cookie?" Jenny asked.

The children all reached for more. Tina bit into her cookie and glanced up at Oak's canopy. She decided she would like Saturdays with her new friends and looked forward to learning more about talking trees.

"Jenny sure tells it well," said Maple. "I don't think I have to worry about how the new owners will take care of me. I enjoy living here."

The calico cat sniffed around for crumbs and then climbed up Oak. He settled on a fat lower branch and stretched himself out along it to sleep. The trees talked some more, but the sound of their voices was lost in the rustling of their leaves. Although the words could not be heard, the trees knew Jenny and the children would be listening.

Copies of this book may be ordered directly from the publisher:

The ISA seal is a registered trademark

International Society of Arboriculture
P. O. Box 3129
Champaign, IL   61826-3129

Phone: (217) 355-9411
Fax: (217) 355-9516
www.ag.uiuc.edu/~isa